CASTLE ADVENTURE
Activity Book

Illustrated by Jen Alliston

Button Books

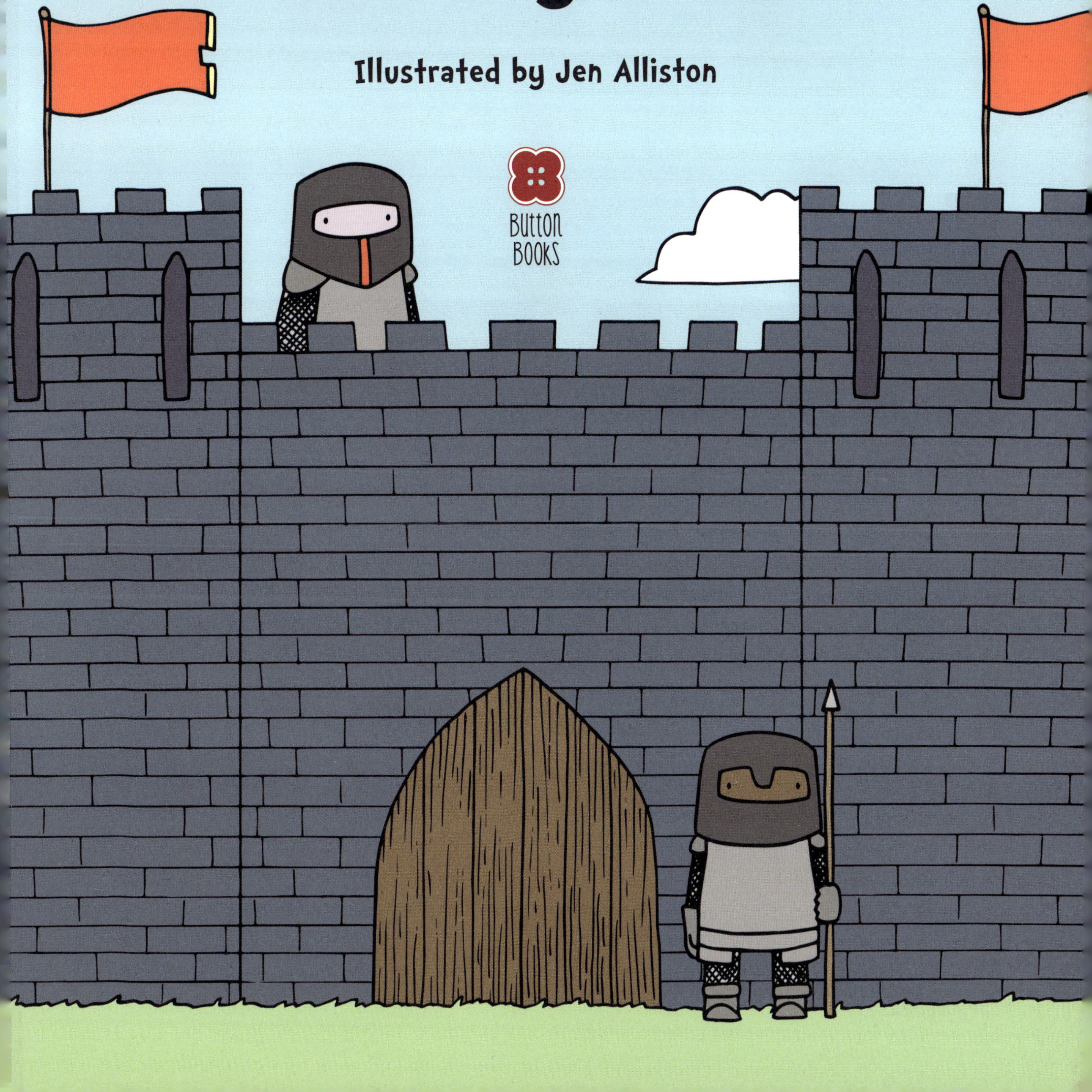

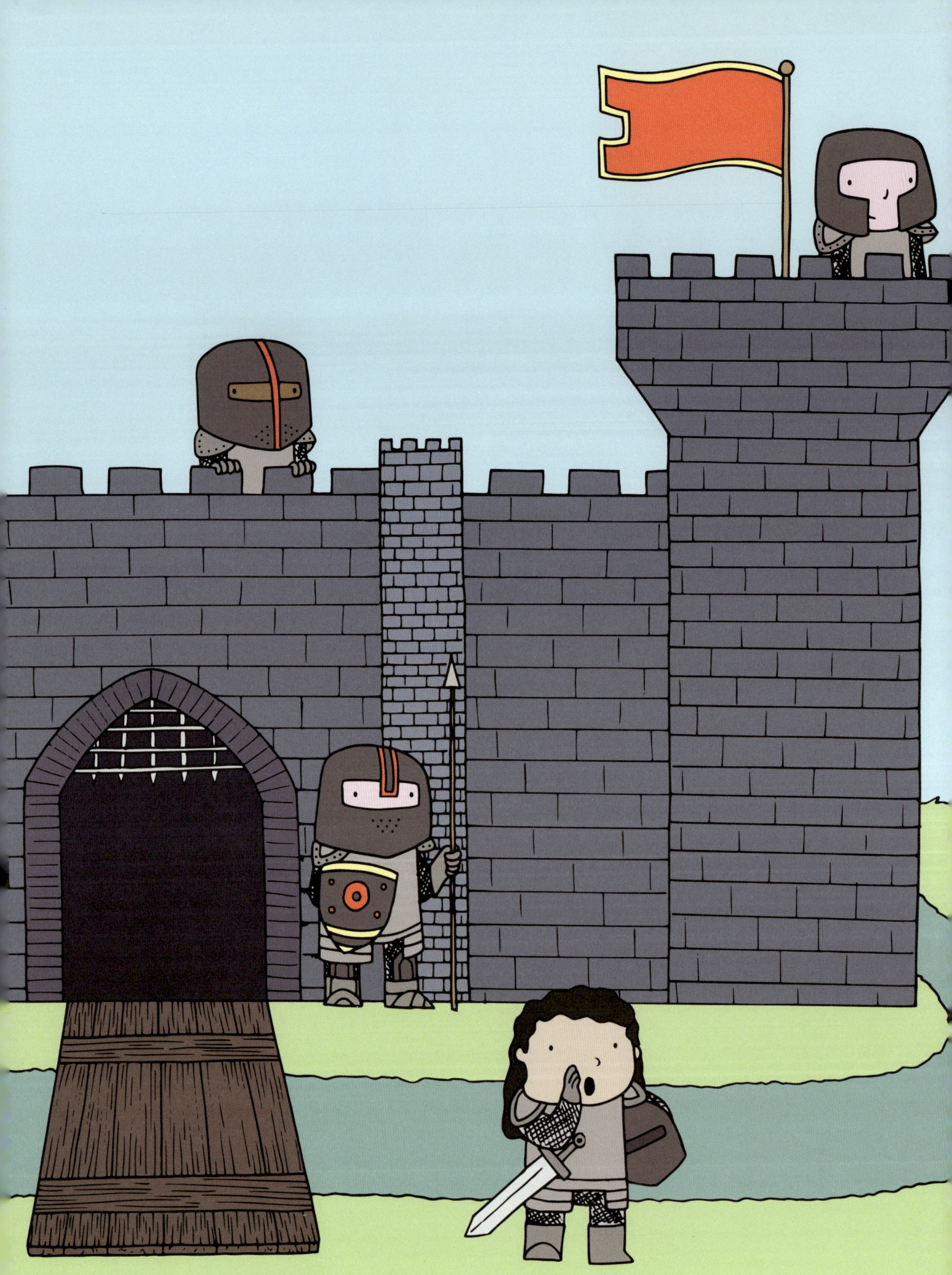

Long ago, in the time known as the Middle Ages, important people lived in castles. These had thick, high walls to protect them. The lord and lady who lived there would have lots of servants and owned the land around their home. When the lord wasn't off fighting in battles he would hold huge feasts and everyone would have a party. So turn the page and let's make merry!

Welcome to the castle!

Use these descriptions to number the different parts of this castle.

1 Battlements
The different heights of stonework mean that soldiers can see out but hide behind the higher parts when they are under attack.

2 Moat
This deep ditch around the castle, often filled with water, makes it difficult for the lord's enemies to get to the castle.

3 Portcullis
This metal gate can be lowered to keep enemies out.

4 Drawbridge
This bridge across the moat can be pulled up if the castle is under attack.

5 Banner
These long flags have patterns that show who lives in the castle.

6 Arrow slits
These narrow openings in the walls let soldiers fire arrows out at attackers without being in danger.

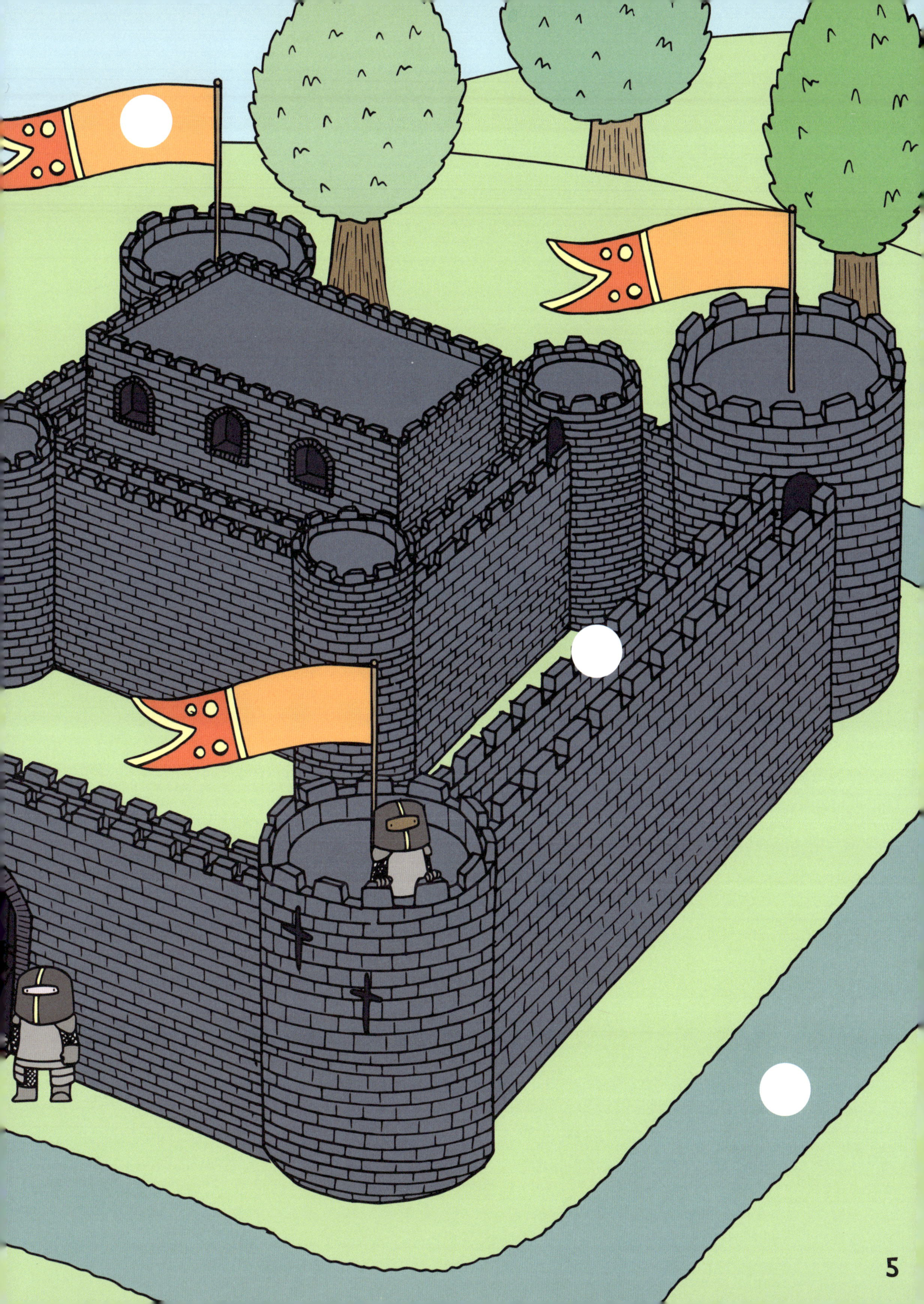

To the rescue

Help the knight to find his way through the forest to rescue the damsel in distress. Be sure to avoid the evil woodcutter and his axe!

Stop, thief!

Which thief stole the knight's arrows? He has a black hat, red boots and blond hair. Can you work out which one he is?

Make a shield

Ask a grown-up to help!

You'll need:

2 sheets of thick cardboard

Paints and paintbrush

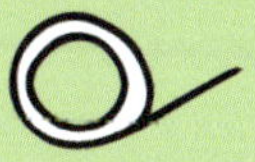

Masking tape

Paper

Ruler

Glue stick

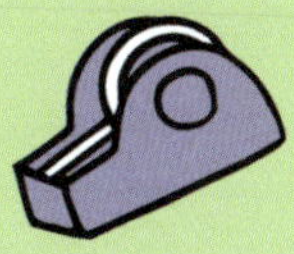

Sticky tape

Scissors

Pencil

1. Draw an outline of a shield on card and cut it out with scissors.

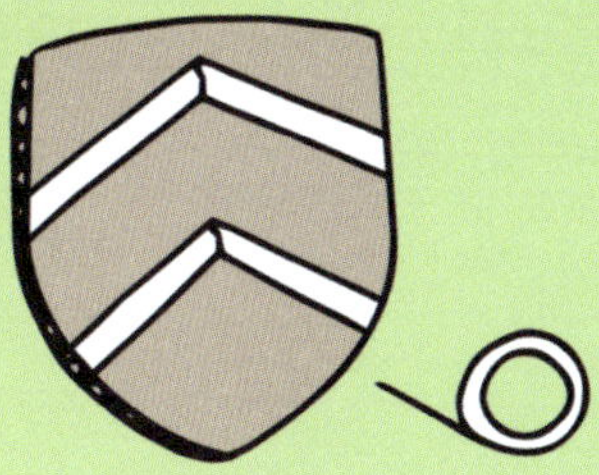

2. Stick on four pieces of masking tape to make a chevron, which is like a bent stripe. This will give you neat edges when you paint it.

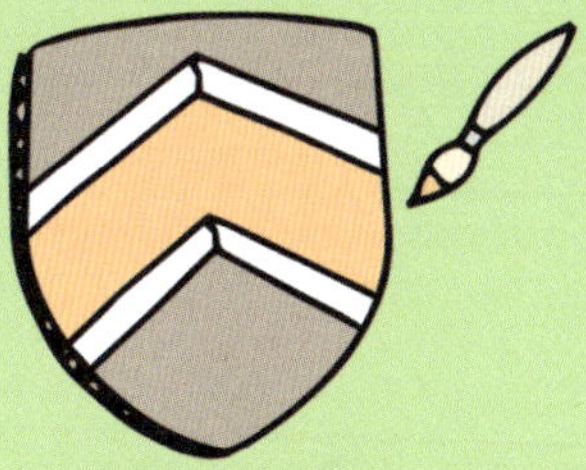

3. Paint the chevron area between the masking tape lines.

4. Remove the tape and paint above and below the chevron, being very careful at the edges.

5. Now you can add decorations, which are called charges. Draw your designs on paper – they can be stars, flowers, animals or anything else you like.

6. Colour them in and cut them out.

7. Stick your charges onto the shield.

8. Now cut out two strips of cardboard about 20 x 5cm to make the arm straps.

9. Tape one end of a strip to the shield, then bend it so it makes a loop that you can put your arm through. Now tape the other end down. Do the same with the other strip. You can wrap more tape round the straps to make them stronger.

10. Now you're protected and ready for battle!

Going to plan

Lots of churches were built in the Middle Ages. This one isn't finished yet. Can you follow the plan to fill in the missing bits and then colour it in?

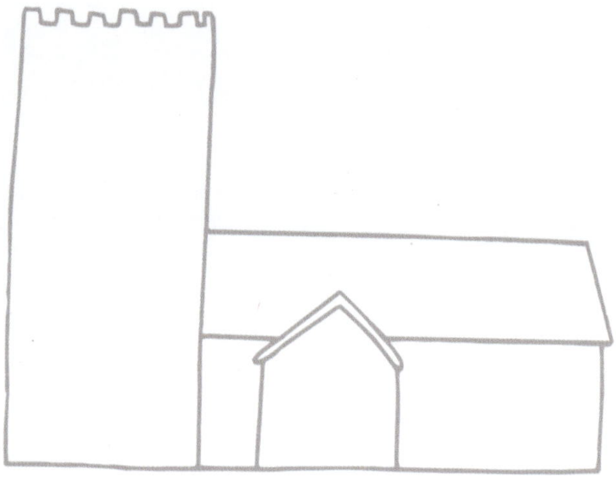

Cart race

Work out the sums to see which cart will deliver its supplies to the castle first. The highest number will get there first.

Create your own medieval adventure

Choose words from the sticker pages to finish this story.

It was Lady Marion's birthday but Sir Jude had gone to [ ] and left her alone at the [ ]. She felt very [ ]. Suddenly she heard the sound of [ ] from the great hall. Opening the [ ] doors, she was amazed to find a huge feast laid out, [ ] playing and all the villagers dancing. When they saw her, they all stopped and shouted: "[ ]!" Then she spotted Sir Jude at the head of the table waiting for her. He had arranged a huge [ ] in her honour, so she had the best birthday ever.

Odd shields out

Can you tell which two shields are the odd ones out? Colour them all in.

Draw a knight's charger

Follow the steps below to draw your own trusty steed.

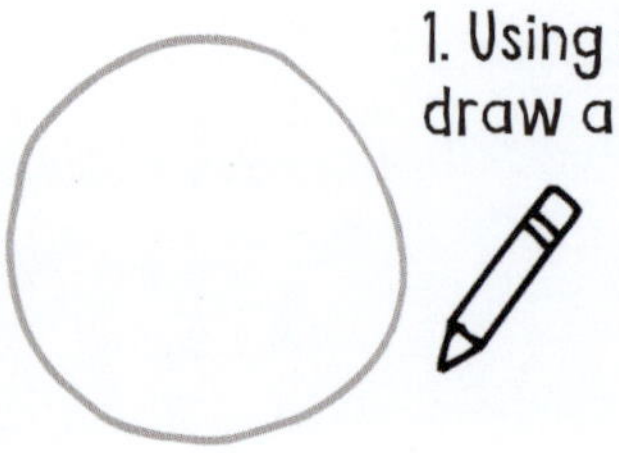

1. Using a pencil, draw a circle.

2. Below the circle draw a neck and add a nose shape to the side.

3. Add an eye, nostrils and ears to your horse.

4. Draw over the main features in pen and add a mane. Now rub out the pencil marks.

Write stuff

Can you spot the five differences between these two scribes?

Home run

This peasant wants to get to her cottage, but she needs to visit the castle on her way. Can you help her through the maze?

Knight jokes

What was Sir Richard's favourite game?

Knights and crosses.

Why were King John's army too tired to fight?
They had lots of sleepless knights.

What do you get when you put a candle in a suit of armour?
A knight light.

Helmet muddle

Can you pair up the helmets and colour them to match?
Can you spot which is the odd one out?

Misty castles

These castles are disappearing into the mist. Complete the outlines and colour them in to make them reappear.

In a spin

Can you spot five differences between these two ladies and their spinning wheels?

Get packing

Sir Jasper is heading off to battle but he's forgotten something. Check the list and work out what's missing.

Sword
Shield
Lance
Cloak
Gloves
Chain mail
Helmet
Boots
Spurs

Defend the castle!

This castle is under attack! Draw more soldiers and use some stickers to add more action to this battle scene.

Make a castle

Ask a grown-up to help!

You'll need:

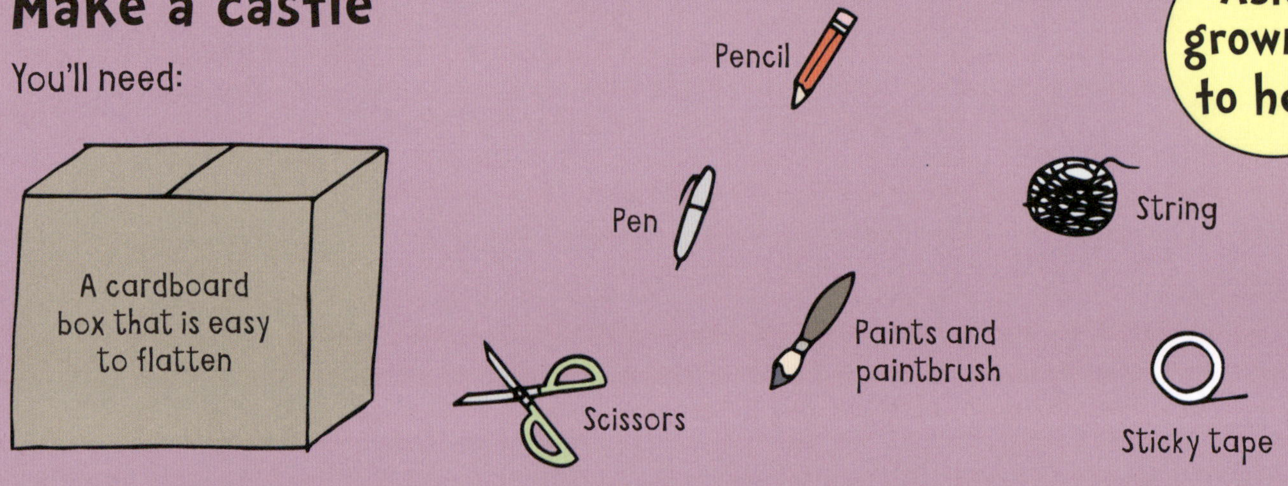

1. Undo the bottom of the box so you can flatten it. Cut the top flaps off.

2. Draw squares around the top of the box to make battlements. Draw a drawbridge on one side.

3. Cut these shapes out, but leave the bottom of the drawbridge attached.

4. Paint the box and leave to dry. Add brick detail with a pen. Stick the box back together with tape.

5. Make a hole either side of the drawbridge with a sharp pencil.

6. Stick the middle of the string to the drawbridge with tape and feed each end of string through the holes.

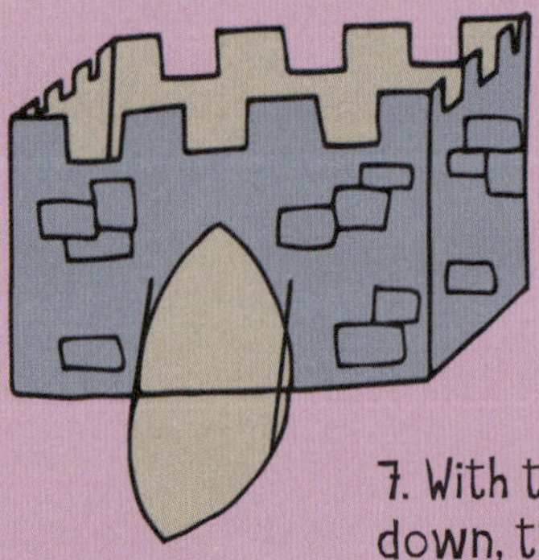

7. With the drawbridge down, tie knots in the string inside the castle.

8. Paint over the tape on the drawbridge and your castle is ready to play with!

Missing tunics

These peasants' tunics have disappeared. Draw them back in and colour them in too. Now count how many feathers in total there are in their caps.

Castle wordsearch

Can you find these hidden castle words?

D	A	E	T	K	H	M	S	J	N	M	D	U	N	G	E	O	N
M	F	I	U	J	M	O	V	G	E	U	E	S	I	C	L	N	X
G	P	O	R	T	C	U	L	L	I	S	G	F	J	O	D	W	C
C	M	H	R	Q	N	Z	T	W	M	K	B	P	G	H	Q	N	T
M	S	F	E	Z	H	P	F	C	L	N	R	X	K	M	P	J	S
Q	Y	T	T	J	R	D	R	A	W	B	R	I	D	G	E	K	T
M	B	D	X	M	T	S	Q	T	P	M	P	U	X	S	T	X	F
E	L	M	G	E	I	M	G	A	T	E	H	O	U	S	E	U	M
H	I	W	R	C	A	O	M	P	B	A	W	Y	F	M	L	T	K
M	O	A	T	U	F	M	K	U	Q	S	G	O	M	I	C	W	E
Q	K	L	L	B	P	J	S	L	M	T	O	W	E	R	J	M	E
W	N	L	M	Q	L	M	K	T	N	E	G	M	P	K	M	N	P

TURRET
PORTCULLIS
TOWER
CATAPULT
MOAT
KEEP
DRAWBRIDGE
WALL
DUNGEON
GATEHOUSE

Battle ready

Can you use these descriptions to number the parts of this suit of armour?

❶ **Helmet**
Protects the head.

❷ **Breastplate**
Protects the chest.

❸ **Greaves**
Protect the shins.

❹ **Gauntlets**
Protect the hands.

❺ **Pauldrons**
Protect the shoulders.

❻ **Cuisses**
Protect the thighs.

Fancy dressing

The queen and her friends are getting ready for a banquet.
Use the stickers to dress them up.

Juggling muddle

These jugglers have dropped everything! Can you work out which three things each juggler was juggling?

Crowning glories

Match these crowns up with the kings and queens by drawing lines to connect them. There is one odd crown out. Which one is it?

Making merry

Why were the early days of history called the Dark Ages?
Because there were so many knights.

How do you find a princess?
You follow the foot prince.

What do you call a device that fills the space beneath the drawbridge?
A remoat control.

Treasure trail

Follow the clues to find where the king's jewels are hidden in this castle that we're looking down on. Draw your route on the picture and mark the spot with an X.

Start in the East tower. Go across the battlements to the South tower. Go down the stairs into the Hall. Go round to the Barrel room and into the Shield room. Go through the Scroll room into the Dining hall and mark your X at the foot of the stairs.

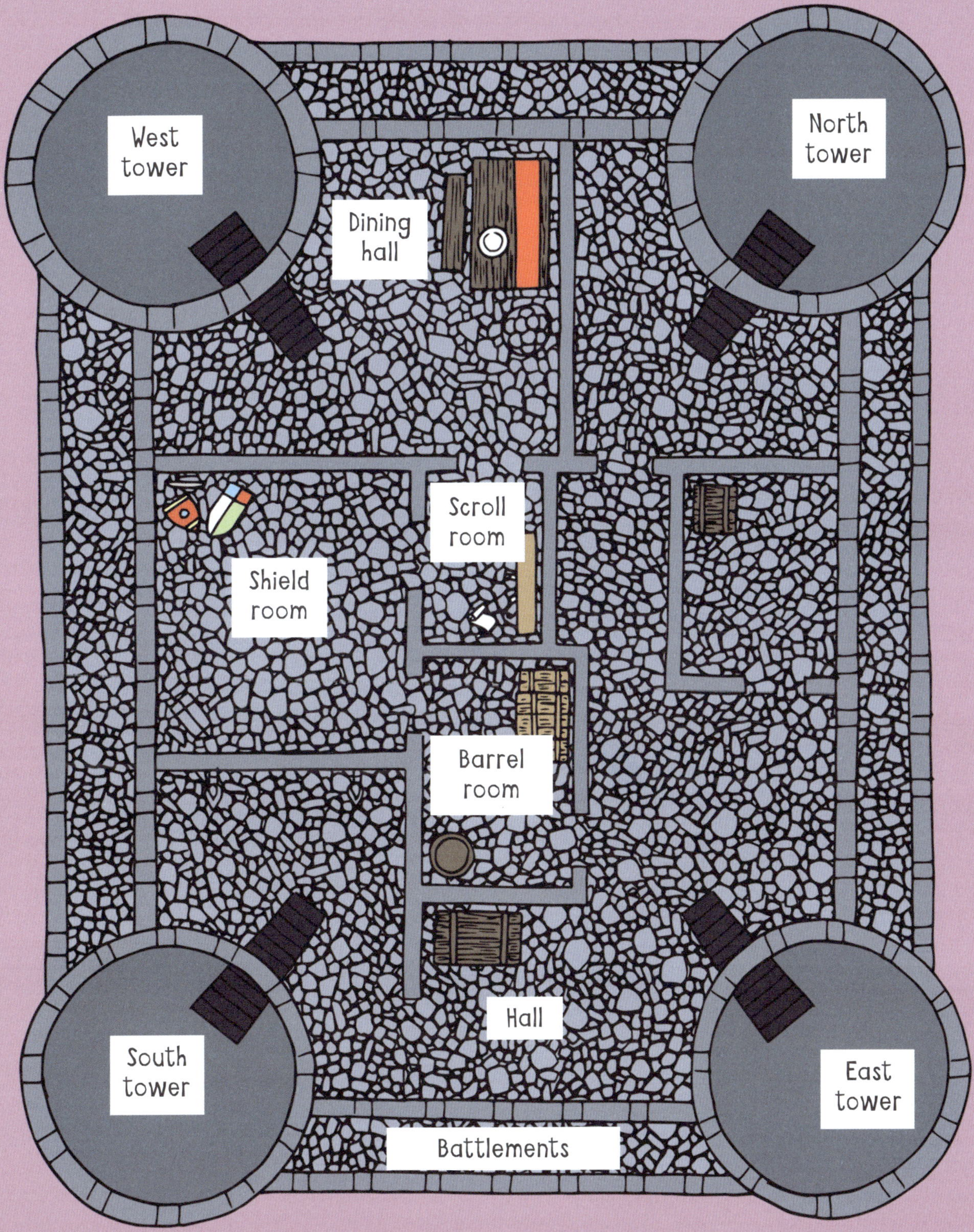

Funny business

Can you tell which jester is the odd one out? Then colour them all in.

Dotty knight

Join the dots to show this brave knight on a charger and colour the picture in.

Make your own coat of arms

Design your own coat of arms on this shield. It can feature stars, lions, dogs or anything else that shows how brave you are.

Muddled up

This silly scribe has got these medieval jobs jumbled up. Can you work out what he should have written?

FABFILI ________

NOMK ______

DREALH _______

SEJERT _______

UEQNE _____

Fabulous feasting

Add some stickers so that everyone has lots to eat at this banquet. The minstrels in the gallery are too faint to be heard. Draw over their outlines and colour them in so they can be seen and heard!

Counting up

The lord has asked the villagers to count up all their animals. Can you help them count how many of each they have?

Pigs =

Sheep =

Chicks =

Ducks =

Cows =

Hens =

Princess party

Colour in these princesses. Which one has the most jewels? Can you put them in height order? Number them from 1 for the smallest to 5 for the tallest.

Horsing around

Can you spot five differences between these two knights' chargers?

Dinner is served

Help this servant to find his way through the castle to the great hall to serve up the platter of food. Go as quickly as you can before the food gets cold!

Country life

Add some stickers to bring this farming scene to life.

Unwanted guests

Rats were everywhere in medieval times! How many can you spot in this castle kitchen?

Shield pairs

Can you spot the pairs of shields? Colour them in to match.

Joust good friends

Which of these knights will win the jousting? He has two feathers on his helmet, a red striped lance and his horse is wearing blue.

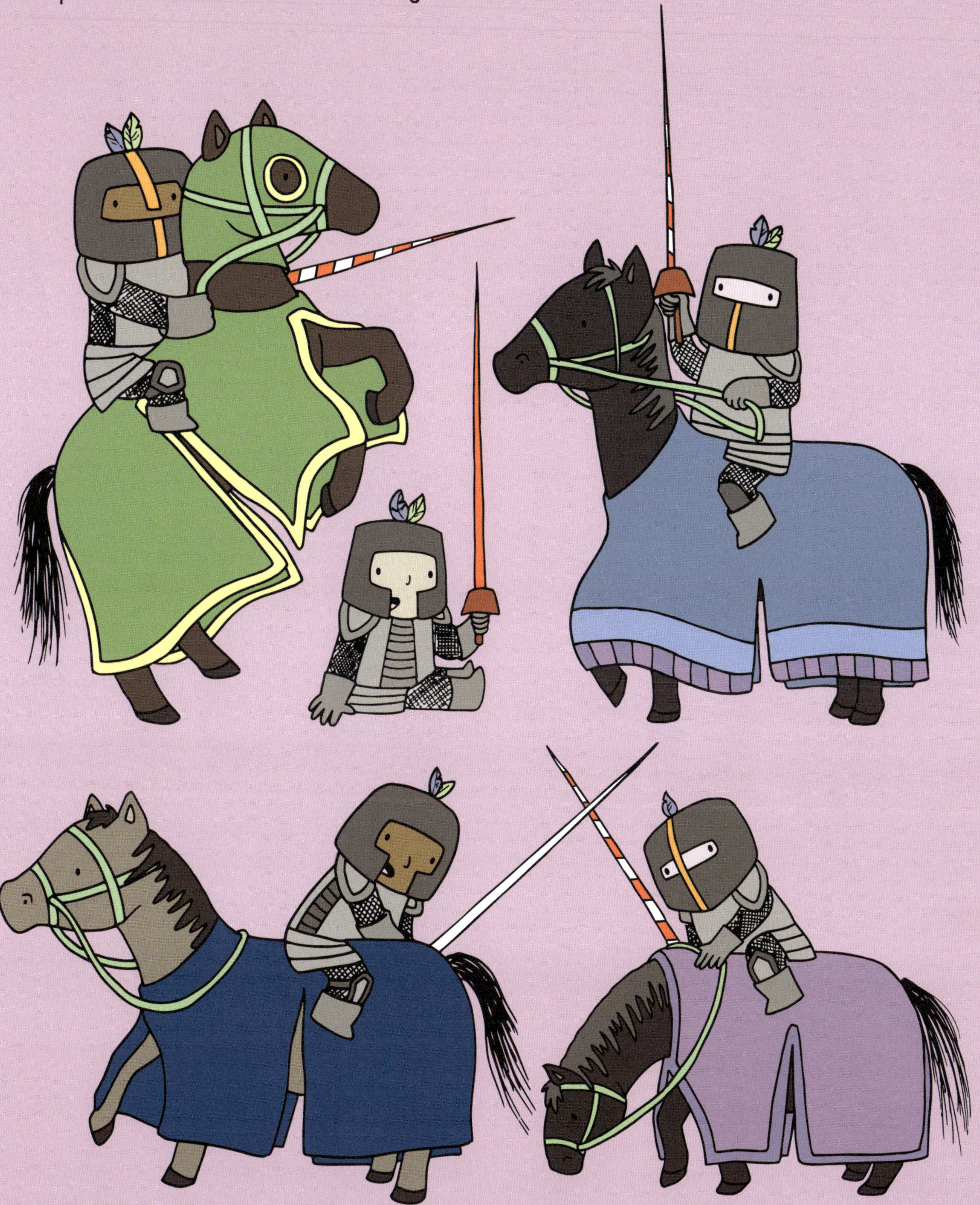

Armour wordsearch

Can you find all the words in the puzzle?

VISOR
HELMET
BREASTPLATE
LANCE
SHIELD
ARROW
GAUNTLET
SWORD

G I Q L F C M G A U N T L E T N E G V Q
A B V M S M D P X E J D P B Q D Y X A C
I M F O H N A K O M N F W G E W M A F K
T R X Q I U R E Q R P S X M S H C R I P
H Q B R E A S T P L A T E U W Y M R S M
X R M P L O R K X A P V G K O B K O E T
P D S D M T M J N Y A X I R M Y W P
J S H M V Q V H C X R S D D B M W E
R G K L H E L M E T Q P D A M B T R
W B N B J F M P Q B N P M Z D O
O H I G M Q K S Z J R G F B B N
X Q R K J T V S G L K P H B
B C X F V I S O R X F D
N L M G X Q D P G R
O P T M R R C T
I O J B G C
L W

Little gems

Princess Matilda wants to share her jewels with Princess Eleanor. How many will they each have if they are divided equally? Colour them red for Matilda and green for Eleanor.

Surprise

music

feast

battle

castle

massive

minstrels

bored

Musical mix-up

These minstrels have got their instruments mixed up. Can you work out which one belongs to which minstrel?

Hidden weapons

This knight has lost his sword, lance, shield, bow and arrow. Can you spot them?

People wordsearch

Can you find these people in the puzzle?

JESTER
SCRIBE
PRINCESS
SHERIFF
BLACKSMITH
CLERK
CARPENTER
PAGE

M	W	X	J	E	S	T	E	R	G	A	X	S
H	Q	R	M	V	H	R	P	M	W	X	Z	O
B	M	P	W	X	E	M	T	C	L	E	R	K
L	D	W	G	M	R	R	P	M	W	X	Z	O
A	M	W	Q	G	I	B	Q	L	T	Q	Z	B
C	P	X	C	M	F	Y	N	V	Q	V	M	R
K	N	M	A	G	F	M	R	J	P	M	Q	Z
S	M	D	R	M	K	H	M	G	Y	M	D	M
M	F	G	P	R	I	N	C	E	S	S	G	Q
I	W	M	E	M	W	X	M	Z	M	C	M	K
T	M	R	N	R	X	M	G	Q	S	R	F	M
H	R	Q	T	M	P	G	Q	K	M	I	Y	X
M	G	L	E	M	F	B	W	M	R	B	Q	K
Y	S	M	R	G	H	Z	P	A	G	E	M	Q
M	G	M	U	F	W	M	X	T	C	M	V	A

Get ahead

These ladies have muddled up their hats. Can you match them up?

Different dungeons

Can you find six differences between these two dungeon pictures?

Hard day's knight

Colour in these different stages of becoming a knight.

Page

Being a page is the first stage a boy goes through if he wants to be a knight.

Squire

As a squire, this older boy looks after a knight and trains for battle.

Knight

The king or queen makes a squire into a knight by touching him on the shoulders with a sword.

Dotty castle

Join the dots to finish this castle picture.

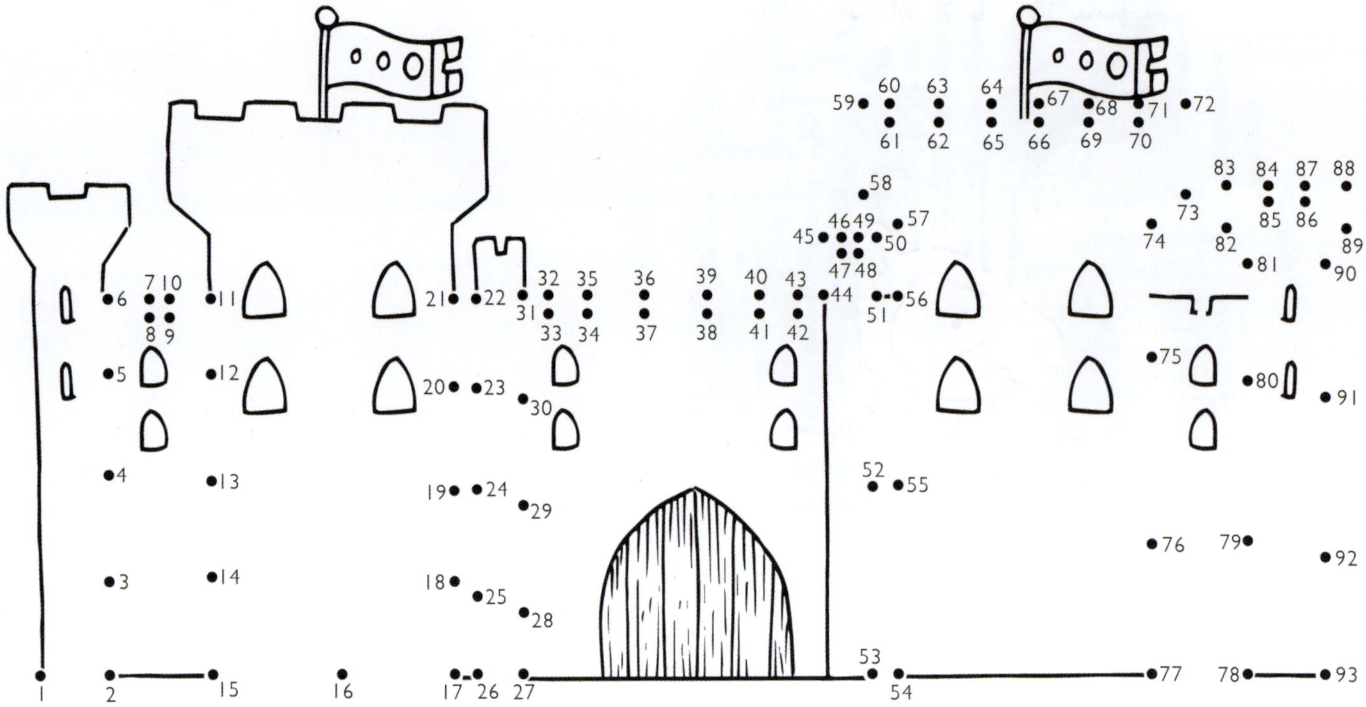

Hidden arrows

These soldiers are practising with their bows and arrows but their aim isn't very good yet. How many arrows have hit the target? And how many arrows they have lost?

Jingle jangle

Colour in this jolly jester and his dog. How many bells can you count on his costume?

Knights in the night

Can you work out which knight matches the shadow?

A stitch in olden times

Help Lady Helen with her embroidery by colouring in the squares according to the key.

- 1 = light blue
- 2 = pale yellow
- 3 = pale green
- 4 = pink
- 5 = purple

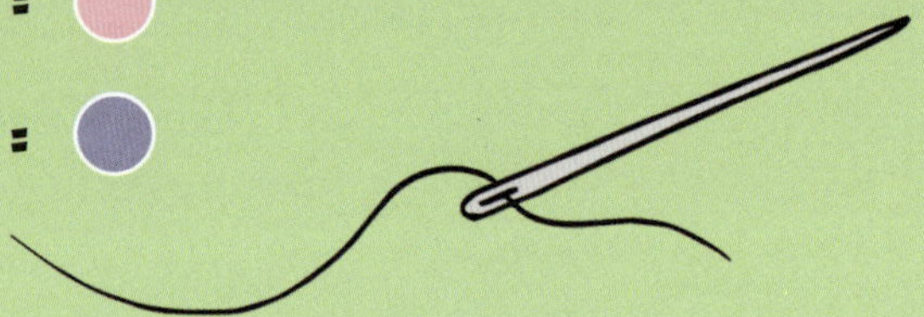

Crowning glory

Follow the steps to draw a crown.

1. Draw an oblong.

2. Draw a curve from one top corner to the other. Add two other curved lines a little distance apart about halfway down the oblong.

3. Draw zigzag lines between the middle curve and the top one. Add circles to the top points.

4. Add curves between each zigzag.

5. Draw the outline of the bottom of the crown.

6. Add jewels and round off the crown details.

7. Go over the details in pen and colour in your crown!

On the battlefield

Can you find the following things in this battle scene?

6 spears
2 axes
3 swords
2 longbows
4 arrows

Make a princess cone hat

Ask a grown-up to help!

You'll need:

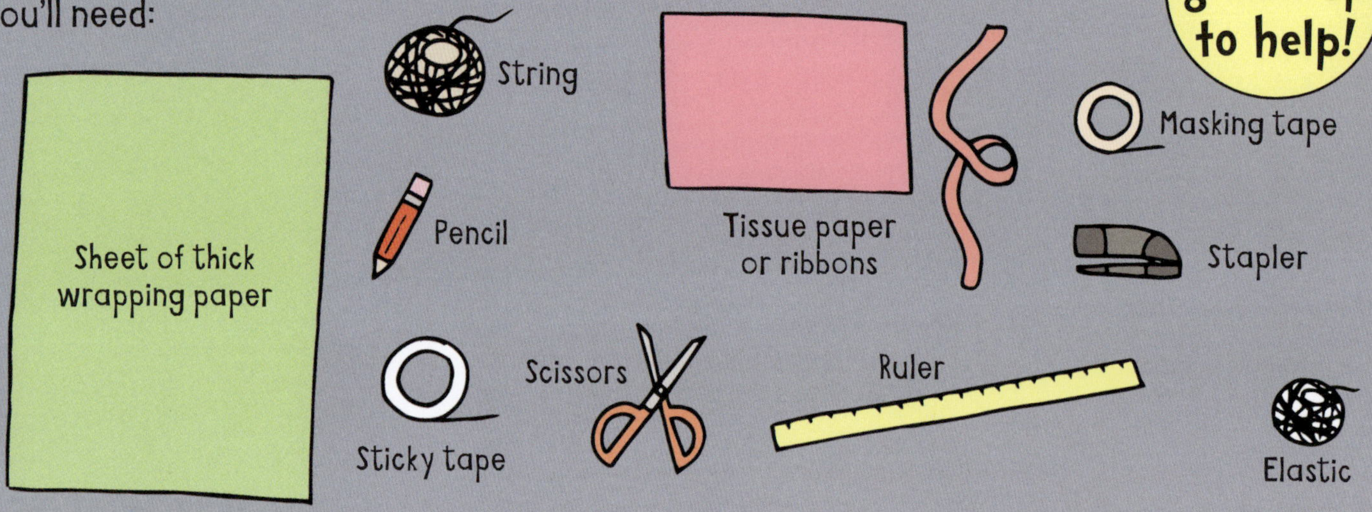

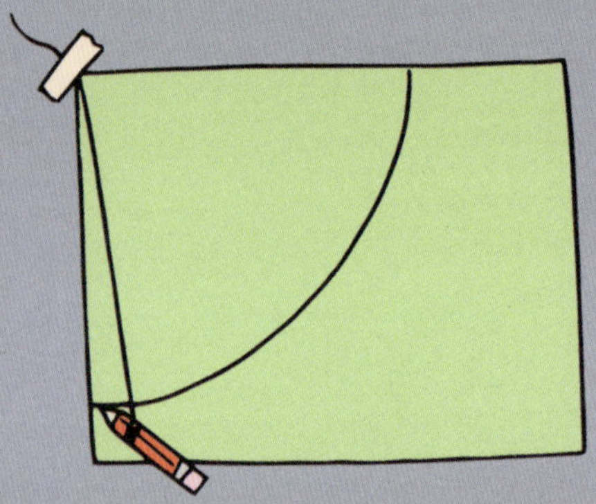

1. Tape one end of the string to a corner of the wrapping paper. Tie the other end of the string to your pencil so that the pencil reaches to the end of the shorter edge. Draw a curve round to the longer edge.

2. Cut the quarter circle shape out with scissors.

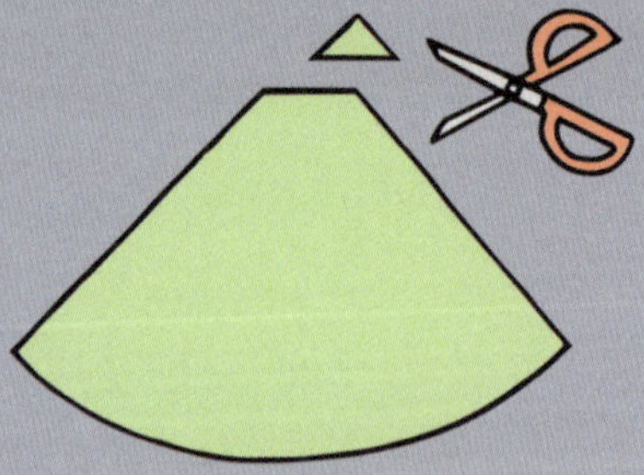

3. Cut the tip of the right angle off.

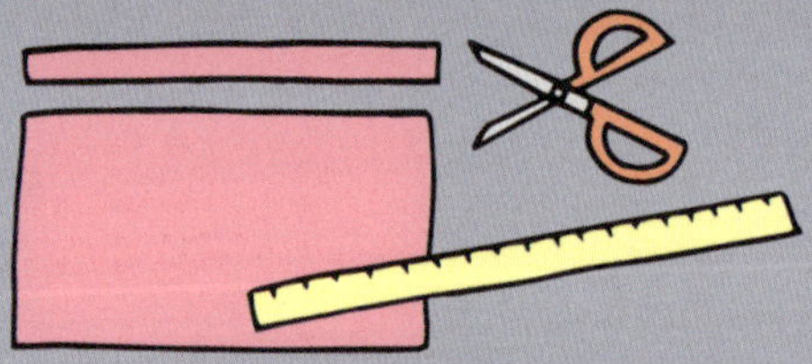

4. Cut the tissue paper into 30cm-long strips, or cut your ribbons to this length.

5. Tape them together to make streamers and stick to where the corner was.

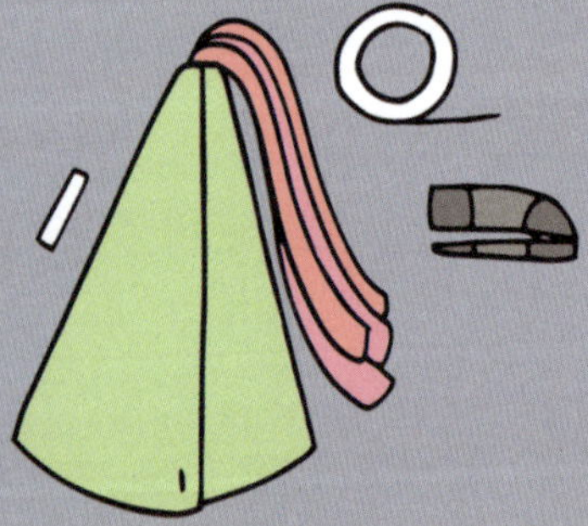

6. Curve your paper into a cone and staple it to the right size for your head. Secure with sticky tape.

7. Make holes either side with the pencil and thread elastic through. Tie knots in the ends.

8. Now wear your princess hat with pride!

Castle under attack

Can you work out which of the catapult stones will hit the castle?

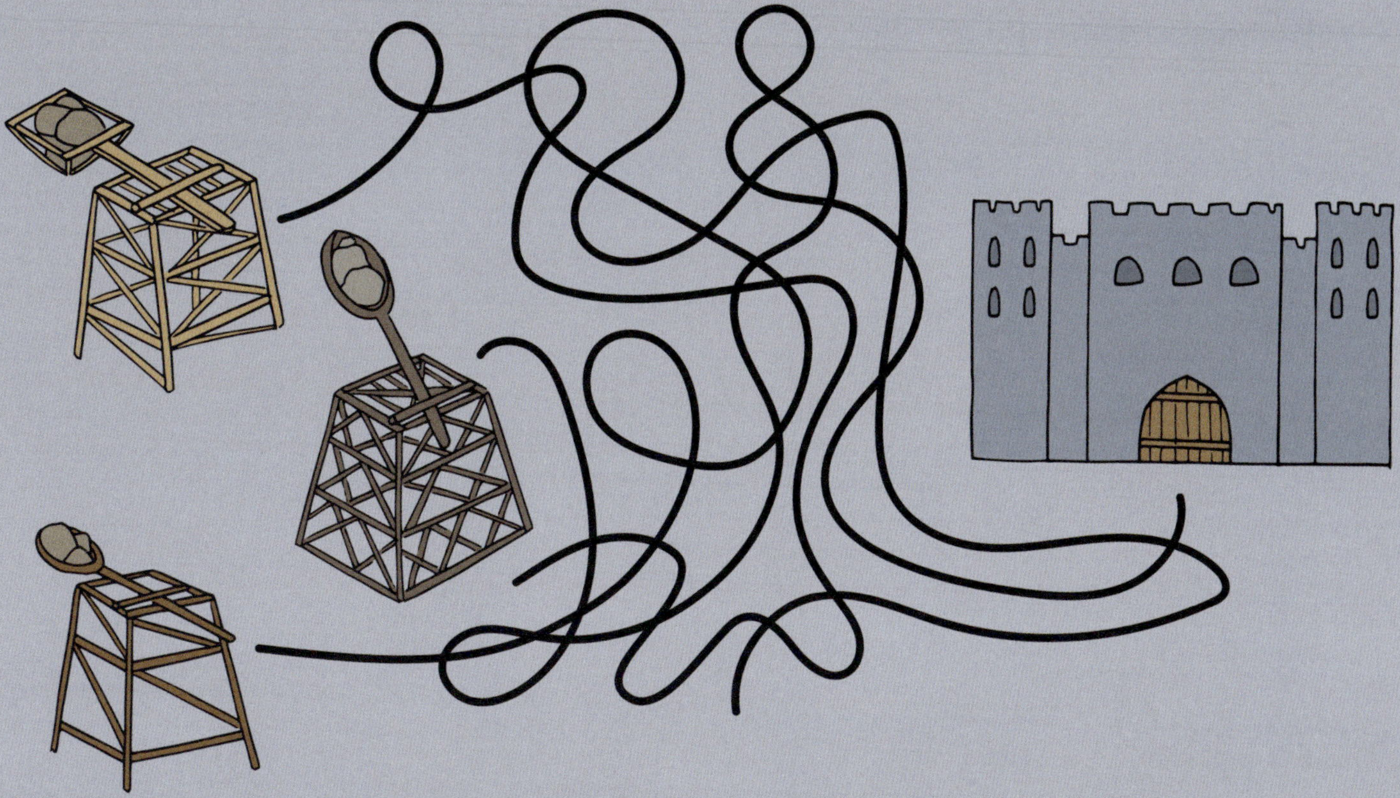

Feast day

The king's cook has forgotten to make some of the king's favourite food. Can you help her by working out which two things she has missed?

Boiled sweets
Pig's head
Sugared almonds
Stew

Bread
Pigeon pie
Roast chicken

Muddled jobs

These medieval craftspeople have got their crafts mixed up. Can you unscramble the letters to work out what they have made?

Blacksmith

ROESHOSHE

Fletcher

RWROA

Carpenter

ATLEB

Candlemaker

ENDALC

Horrible diseases wordsearch

There were lots of nasty illnesses in medieval times. Can you find these ones? (But don't catch them!)

LEPROSY
FLU
CHOLERA
SMALLPOX
MEASLES
PLAGUE
SCURVY

K	L	Y	N	C	H	O	L	E	R	A	R	M
M	F	R	P	W	M	Z	Q	M	X	D	V	E
G	T	P	C	X	R	S	Q	Z	T	J	M	A
M	R	B	G	Q	C	Z	V	P	W	X	M	S
T	W	K	S	M	A	L	L	P	O	X	C	L
M	H	M	C	X	M	E	M	H	G	T	P	E
C	X	R	U	M	Q	P	G	T	P	M	Z	S
Q	T	M	R	B	M	R	C	X	R	Y	M	V
G	T	P	V	Q	R	O	M	R	C	X	R	P
M	Z	Q	Y	M	X	S	G	T	P	R	F	R
G	T	P	X	R	P	Y	M	C	X	R	L	M
M	C	X	R	G	T	R	P	L	A	G	U	E

Well-dressed lady

Can you use these descriptions to label the different items of clothing this lady is wearing?

❶ Smock
Made of white linen or silk, this was worn next to the skin.

❷ Hose
These kept the lady's feet and legs warm.

❸ Kirtle
This long dress was worn over the smock and often laced up at the front or side.

❹ Girdle
This belt was often very decorative.

❺ Surcoat
Worn over the lady's other clothes, these often had no sleeves.

❻ Hennin
These pointed hats often had veils coming out of the top.

Jousting fun

Colour in this jousting tournament picture. Can you spot a juggler, jester, page, minstrel, king and queen?

Castle confusion

Sir Percival wants to visit his friend Lord Richard but he can't remember where he lives! Can you help him work out which castle Richard lives in? It has two flags, six windows and two doorways.

On the hunt

It's the castle cat's job to find mice. Which way should she go to catch the mouse? Make sure you avoid the dogs!

What's cooking?

These two cooks look very similar but there are five differences. Can you spot them?

Counting out

Sir Hugh has a lot of different weapons. Can you count up how many he has of each?

Swords =

Arrows =

Lances =

Medieval decor

Colour in the tapestry to help Sir Edward and Lady Isabella decorate their castle. How many trees are there?

Silly knights

What is the name of the knight who enjoys practical jokes?
Sir Prize

Which knight is always sure about things?
Sir Tanlee

Which knight is the roundest at the table?
Sir Cumference

Which knight is good at doing operations?
Sir Jun

Which knight is always still standing after a battle?
Sir Vivor

Taking aim

Which arrow will hit the target? Work out the sums on each arrow to see which one matches the target.

Dotty battle

Join the dots to complete this picture.

Make a sword

Ask a grown-up to help!

You'll need:

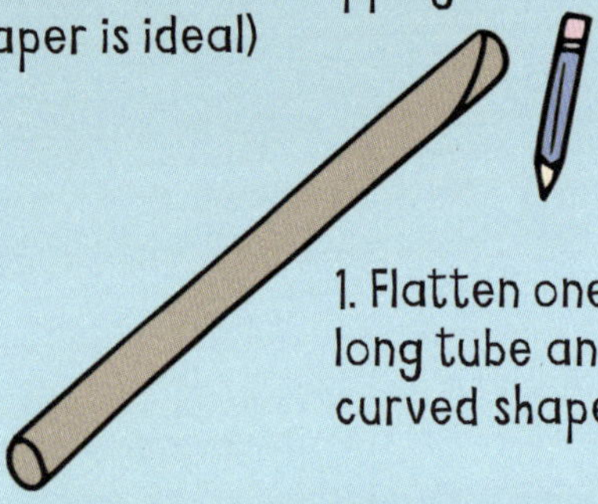

1. Flatten one end of the long tube and draw a curved shape at the end.

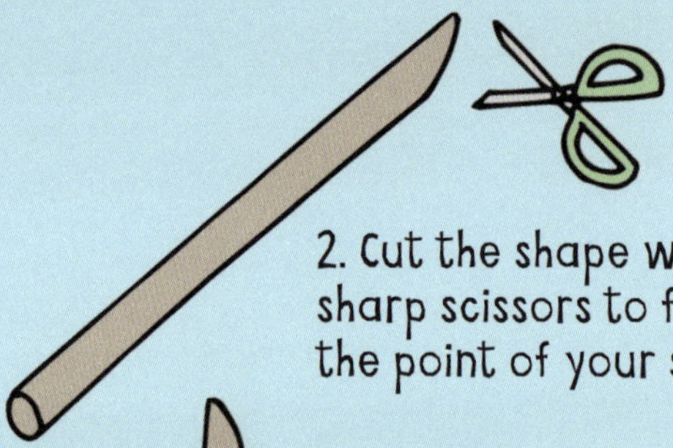

2. Cut the shape with sharp scissors to form the point of your sword.

3. Cut a strip of card from a cereal packet about 22cm long and wider than the diameter of the tube.

4. Stand the non-pointed end of the tube at one end of the strip of card and draw round it.

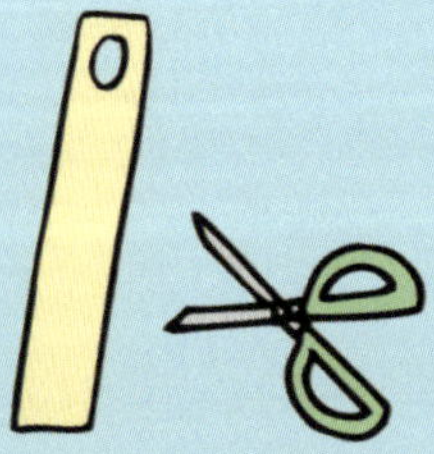

5. Cut this circle out, then cut your strip so that it is about 1cm wider than the hole on both sides.

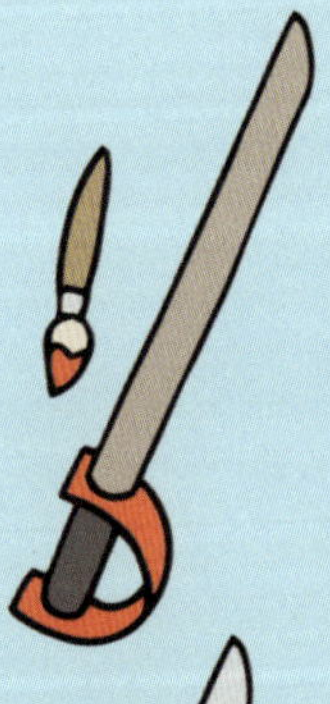

6. Paint one side of the strip and slip the tube through the hole. Bend the card over, with the painted side outwards, and position it so that it forms a guard for your hand. Check there is enough space for you to hold the handle, then glue the strip to the end of the tube.

7. Wrap the blade in foil, securing it with sticky tape at the top and bottom.

8. Decorate the hand guard with stickers or gems and you're ready to go into battle!

Tall order

The princess is trapped in the tower, which is 10 metres high. The prince has come to save her but can't work out which of his ladders is long enough. Work out the sums to help the prince choose the longest ladder so he can reach the princess without disturbing the sleeping guards. Once she's safe, you can colour in the guards to wake them up!

Stepping out

In medieval times, rich men wore very long pointy shoes. Work out these sums to find out whose shoes are the longest.

3 + 6 + 4 =   5 + 9 – 4 =   3 + 8 + 1 =

Walk in the woods

This servant girl is walking to the castle through the forest. She wants to visit her mother's cottage on the way. Help her find her way, but make sure she avoids the wolves!

Falconry fun

These pictures of two ladies and their falcons look the same, but can you spot five differences between them?

Secret message

The king is worried his enemies are nearby, so has sent Sir Gerard a secret message. Some of the words have been scrambled. Can you work out what the message says?

Help!

Our C_S _ LE is under TH_E_T.
Bring C_T_P__TS and L_DD_R_.

Please muster as many good S_LD_ERS as you can and come Q_IC_LY!

SOLDIERS
CATAPULTS
CASTLE
LADDERS
THREAT
QUICKLY

Motte and bailey

Motte-and-bailey castles consisted of a mound called the motte, with the castle on top, and a courtyard called the bailey. The bailey was full of buildings and bustling with people and animals. Add some stickers to bring this scene to life.

Joust for fun

One of these knights is losing the jousting contest and fading fast! Draw over the outline and colour him in to give him a fighting chance.

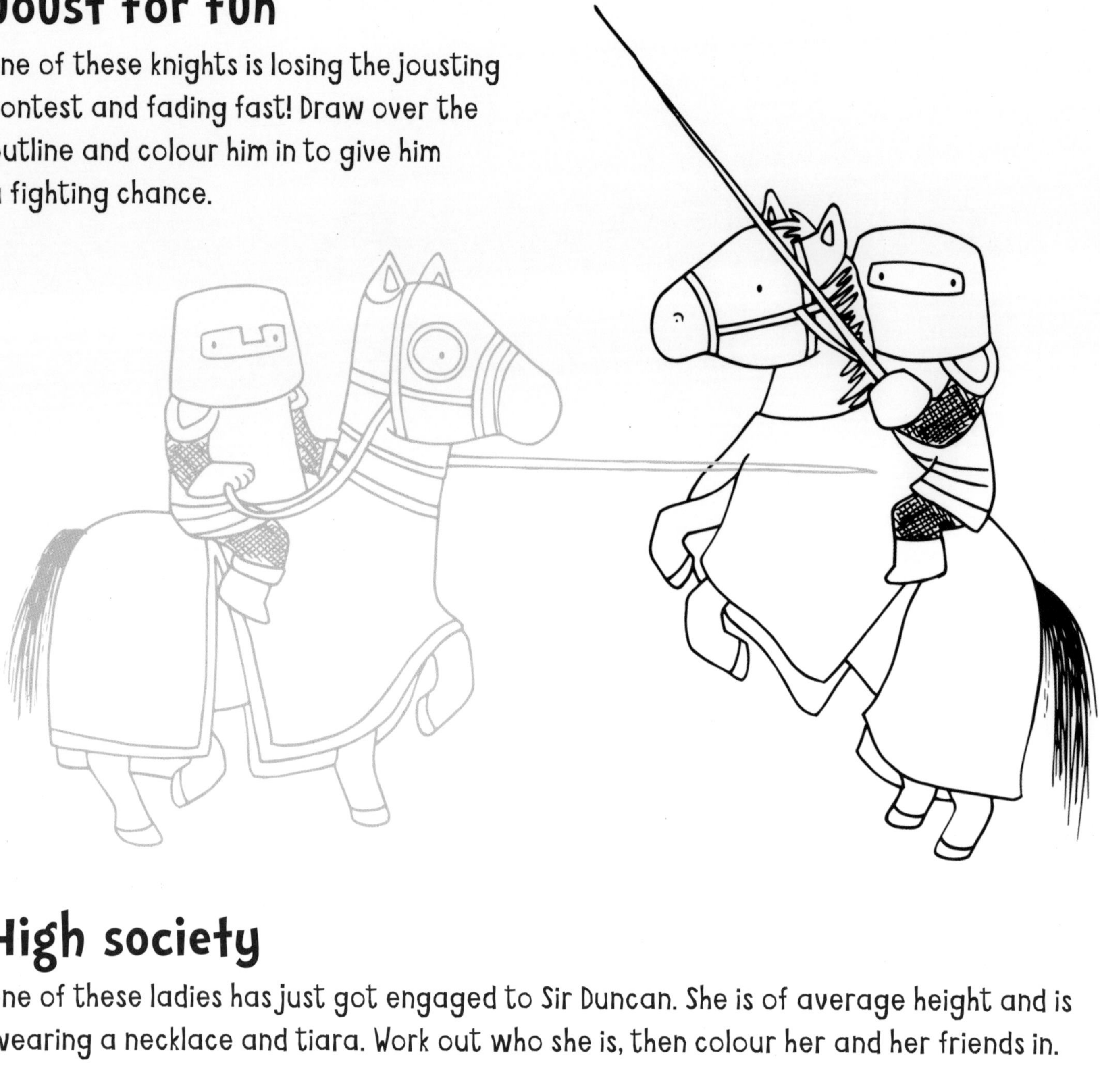

High society

One of these ladies has just got engaged to Sir Duncan. She is of average height and is wearing a necklace and tiara. Work out who she is, then colour her and her friends in.

Hide and seek

The king's hunting party has just been past, so all the forest animals have hidden. Now the hunters are back at the castle, how many creatures can you spot? Then use stickers to add some more.

Welcome to the castle! (pages 4–5)

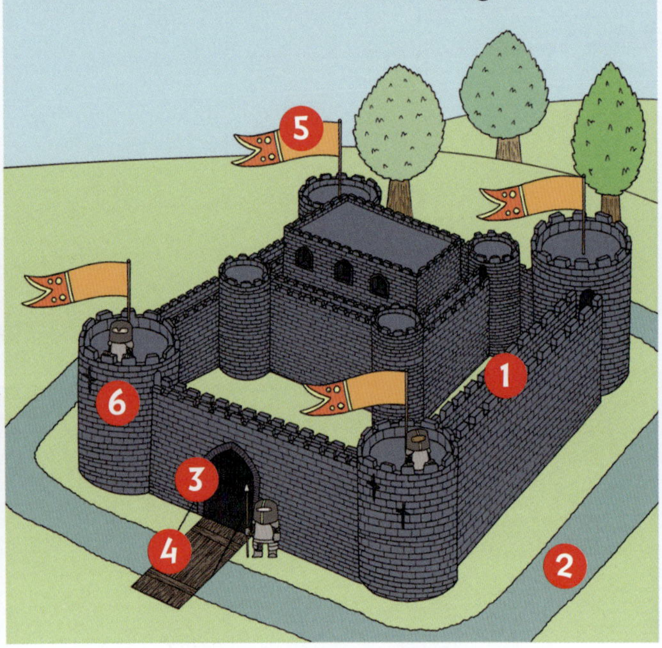

To the rescue (page 6)

Stop, thief! (page 6)

Cart race (page 8)

Odd shields out (page 9)

Write stuff (page 10)

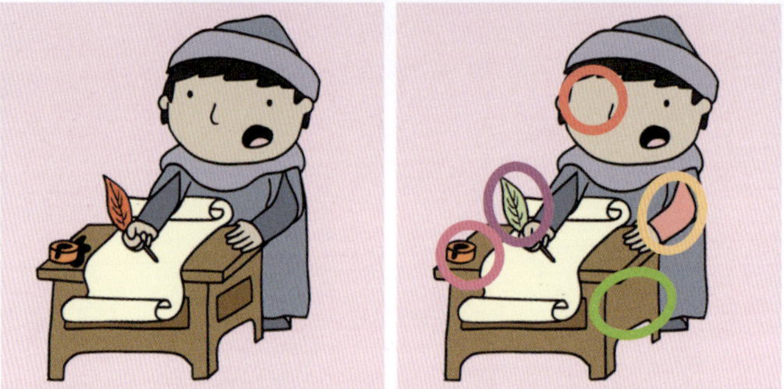

Home run (page 11)

Helmet muddle (page 12)

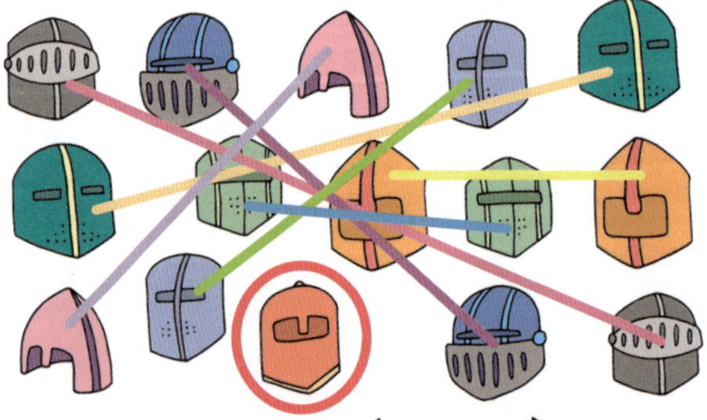

In a spin (page 13)

Get packing (page 13)

The boots are missing

Missing tunics (page 17)

There are 14 feathers in the peasants' caps

Castle wordsearch (page 17)

D	A	E	T	K	H	M	S	J	N	M	D	U	N	G	E	O	N
M	F	I	U	J	M	O	V	G	E	U	E	S	I	C	L	N	X
G	P	O	R	T	C	U	L	L	I	S	G	F	J	O	D	W	C
C	M	H	R	Q	N	Z	T	W	M	K	B	P	G	H	Q	N	T
M	S	F	E	Z	H	P	F	C	L	N	R	X	K	M	P	J	S
Q	Y	T	T	J	R	D	R	A	W	B	R	I	D	G	E	K	T
M	B	D	X	M	T	S	Q	T	P	M	P	U	X	S	T	X	F
E	L	M	G	E	I	M	G	A	T	E	H	O	U	S	E	U	M
H	I	W	R	C	A	O	M	P	B	A	W	Y	F	M	L	T	K
M	O	A	T	U	F	M	K	U	Q	S	G	O	M	I	C	W	E
Q	K	L	L	B	P	J	S	L	M	T	O	W	E	R	J	M	E
W	N	L	M	Q	L	M	K	T	N	E	G	M	P	K	M	N	P

Battle ready (page 18)

Juggling muddle (page 19)

Crowning glories (page 20)

Treasure trail (page 21)

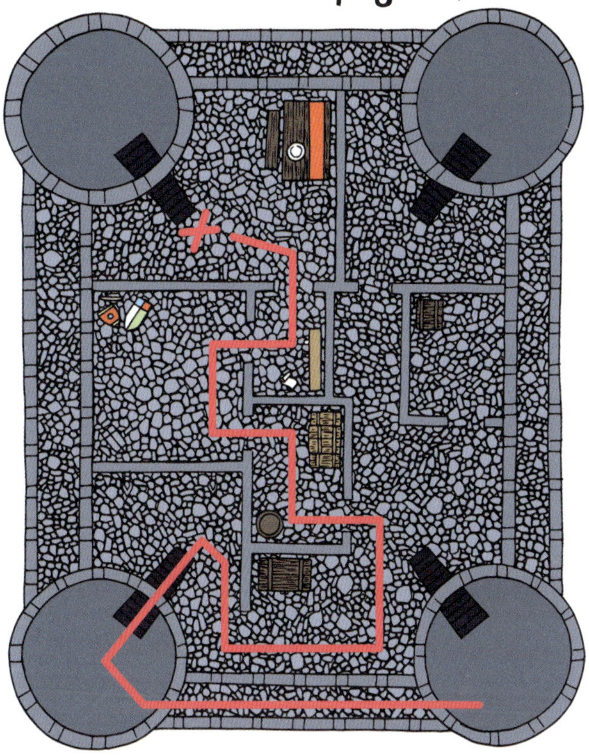

Funny business (page 22)

Muddled up (page 23)

Counting up (page 26)

Pigs = 4
Sheep = 3
Chicks = 2
Ducks = 2
Cows = 1
Hens = 3

Princess party (page 26)

Horsing around (page 27)

Dinner is served (page 27)

Unwanted guests (page 30)

There are 10 rats

Shield pairs (page 30)

Joust good friends (page 31)

Armour wordsearch (page 32)

G I Q L F C M G A U N T L E T N E G V Q
A B I M S M D P X E J D P B Q D Y X A C
I M F O H N A K O M N F W G E W M A F K
T R X Q I U R E Q R P S X M S H C R I P
H Q B R E A S T P L A T E U W Y M R S M
E M P L O R K X A P V G K O B K O E T
P D S D M T M J N Y A X I R M Y W P
J S H M V Q V H C X R S D D B M W E
R G K L H E L M E T Q P D A M B A R
W O N B J F M P Q B N P M Z D O
O H I G M Q K E Z J R G F B B N
X Q R K J T V S G L K P H B
B C A F V I S O R I H O
N L M G X Q D P G R
O P T M R R C T
I O J B G A
L W

Little gems (page 32)

They get 7 gems each

Musical mix-up (page 33)

Hidden weapons (page 33)

People wordsearch (page 34)

M	W	X	J	E	S	T	E	R	G	A	X	S
H	Q	R	M	V	H	R	P	M	W	X	Z	O
B	M	P	W	X	E	M	T	C	L	E	R	K
L	D	W	G	M	R	R	P	M	W	X	Z	O
A	M	W	Q	G	I	B	Q	L	T	Q	Z	B
C	P	X	C	M	F	Y	N	V	Q	V	M	R
K	N	M	A	G	F	M	R	J	P	M	Q	Z
S	M	D	R	M	K	H	M	G	Y	M	D	M
M	F	G	P	R	I	N	C	E	S	S	G	Q
I	W	M	E	M	W	X	M	Z	M	C	M	K
T	M	R	N	R	X	M	G	Q	S	R	F	M
H	R	Q	T	M	P	G	Q	K	M	I	Y	X
M	G	L	E	M	F	B	W	M	R	B	Q	K
Y	S	M	R	G	H	Z	P	A	G	E	M	Q
M	G	M	U	F	W	M	X	T	C	M	V	A

Get ahead (page 34)

Different dungeons (page 35)

Hidden arrows (page 36)

Jingle jangle (page 37)

There are 11 bells

Knights in the night (page 37)

A stitch in olden times (page 38)

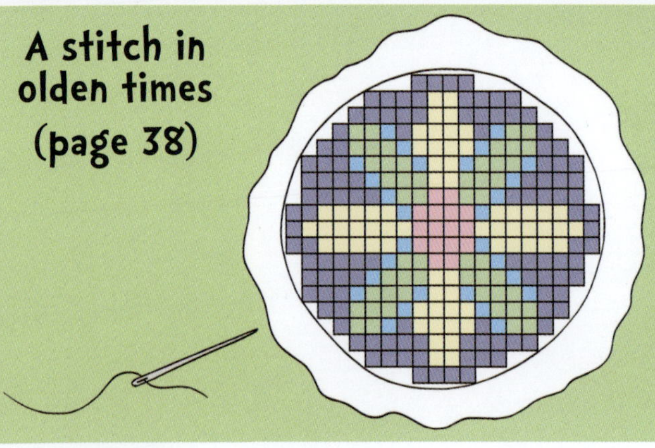

On the battlefield (page 39)

Castle under attack (page 41)

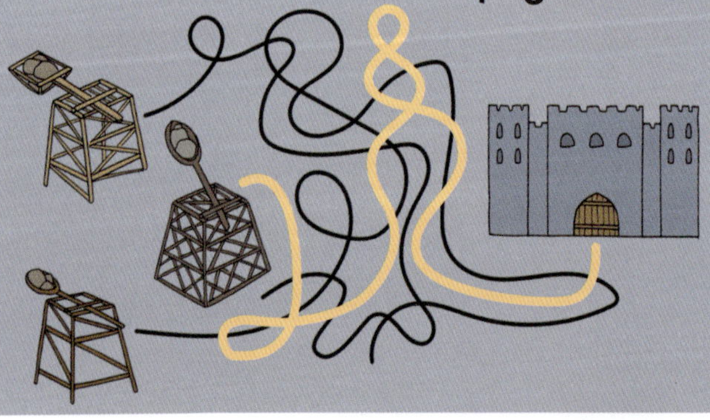

Feast day (page 41)

The sugared almonds and roast chicken are missing

Muddled jobs (page 42)

Horrible diseases wordsearch (page 42)

K	L	Y	N	C	H	O	L	E	R	A	R	M
M	F	R	P	W	M	Z	Q	M	X	D	V	E
G	T	P	C	X	R	S	Q	Z	T	J	M	A
M	R	B	G	Q	C	Z	V	P	W	X	M	S
T	W	K	S	M	A	L	L	P	O	X	C	L
M	H	M	C	X	M	E	M	H	G	T	P	E
C	X	R	U	M	Q	P	G	T	P	M	Z	S
Q	T	M	R	B	M	R	C	X	R	Y	M	V
G	T	P	V	Q	R	O	M	R	C	X	R	P
M	Z	Q	Y	M	X	S	G	T	P	R	F	R
G	T	P	X	R	P	Y	M	C	X	R	L	M
M	C	X	R	G	T	R	P	L	A	G	U	E

Well-dressed lady (page 43)

Jousting fun (pages 44–5)

Castle confusion (page 46)

On the hunt (page 46)

What's cooking? (page 47)

Counting out (page 47)

Swords = 2 Arrows = 5 Lances = 3

Medieval decor (page 48)

There are 6 trees

Taking aim (page 49)

Tall order (page 51)

The ladder on the right is long enough to reach the princess.

Stepping out (page 52)

Walk in the woods (page 52)

Falconry fun (page 53)

Secret message (page 53)

Help! Our CASTLE is under THREAT. Bring CATAPULTS and LADDERS. Please muster as many good SOLDIERS as you can and come QUICKLY!

High society (page 56)

Hide and seek (page 57)

There are 7 hidden creatures

First published 2018 by Button Books, an imprint of Guild of Master Craftsman Publications Ltd, Castle Place, 166 High Street, Lewes, East Sussex BN7 1XU, UK. Text © GMC Publications Ltd, 2018. Copyright in the Work © GMC Publications Ltd, 2018. Illustrations © 2018 Jennifer Alliston. ISBN 978 1 78708 020 1.

A catalogue record for this book is available from the British Library. Publisher: Jonathan Bailey. Production: Jim Bulley and Jo Pallett. Senior Project Editor: Wendy McAngus. Managing Art Editor: Gilda Pacitti. Colour origination by GMC Reprographics. Printed and bound in China.